Architecture of Civic Coherence Under Law

Think and Grow Together, Volume 6

Dwight Vaughn

Published by Dwight Vaughn, 2025.

ARCHITECTURE OF CIVIC COHERENCE UNDER LAW

First edition. December 19, 2025.

ISBN: 979-8233112980

Written by Dwight Vaughn.

Dusty

Matt Horning

Ted Joslin

"Coherence is the discipline of restraint."

"Authority endures only where correction remains possible."

"Power fails not when it acts, but when it forgets how to stop."

Architecture of Civic Coherence Under Law

PREFACE

This book exists to address a single, systemic failure in modern governance: the quiet inversion of meaning, authority, and outcome. Across institutions, policies increasingly stabilize processes rather than serve purpose, allowing power and resources to move while accountability erodes. This work does not argue for ideological positions or specific policy outcomes. Instead, it establishes a constitutional, falsifiable framework for restoring alignment—so that authority remains bounded, outcomes remain measurable, and correction occurs before failure becomes crisis. The goal is not control, but coherence.

GLOSSARY

Anchor

The controlling civic reference for legitimacy and constraint: the Declaration of Independence, the Constitution, and the Preamble.

Meaning

The intended real-world condition a policy is designed to produce.

Policy

The authority structure and rules created to pursue Meaning.

Flow

The movement of money, enforcement, incentives, and operational force.

Neutral Baseline (0)

The default posture of constitutional restraint and due process.

Misalignment (−1)

A detectable contradiction between Meaning, Authority, and Flow.

Validated Alignment (+1)

A temporary state where authority is bounded, flow is traceable, and outcomes meet or improve toward defined thresholds.

Correction Cycle

A bounded process (≤ 90 days) to redesign or constrain misaligned action.

Coherence

The degree to which Meaning, Authority, and Flow remain non-contradictory over time.

GLOSSY INDEX (TERMS OF REFERENCE)

Authority, bounded

Correction, fast-fail

Delegation, sunset

Emergency powers

Flow traceability

Neutral baseline

Outcome variance
Separation of powers
Trinary framework

Introduction

Modern governance does not fail loudly. It fails quietly, through accumulation. Programs persist after their purpose has faded, authority expands without clear limits, and resources continue to move long after outcomes stop improving. The result is a system that appears functional while drifting further from its stated goals. This book begins from a simple observation: most public failures are not caused by bad intentions or isolated corruption, but by structural misalignment between meaning, authority, and action.

At the founding of the United States, governance was designed as a constrained system. Power was divided, authority was temporary, and legitimacy depended on consent and clarity of purpose. The Constitution assumed that error was inevitable, which is why it embedded correction mechanisms—checks, balances, sunsets, and review. Over time, those mechanisms weakened. Not through formal repeal, but through normalization of exception, procedural substitution for accountability, and the gradual inversion of decision order. Resources began to flow before purpose was clearly defined, policies adapted to justify that flow, and meaning was rewritten after the fact.

This inversion is now the dominant operating mode of modern institutions. Funding stabilizes systems regardless of performance. Emergency powers outlive emergencies. Regulatory structures optimize for compliance rather than outcomes. Review occurs only after failure becomes systemic. None of this requires conspiracy. It emerges naturally when systems reward continuity more than correction. Once flow becomes self-justifying, alignment becomes optional.

The purpose of this book is not to argue for specific political positions, policies, or ideological outcomes. It does not propose new rights, expand executive power, or rewrite the Constitution. Instead, it asks a more fundamental question: how should decisions be structured so that purpose remains clear, authority remains bounded, outcomes remain measurable, and failure is corrected before it becomes permanent? The answer offered here is not philosophical. It is structural.

This work introduces a trinary governance framework grounded entirely in civic foundations: the Declaration of Independence, the Constitution, and the Preamble. Within this framework, meaning defines intent, authority grants permission, and action produces outcomes. Each element is constrained, observable, and subject to review. Misalignment is treated not as moral failure, but as a detectable system state that requires reversion to neutrality before validation can occur. Progress is earned, temporary, and always reversible.

What follows is an attempt to make governance falsifiable. To define conditions under which policies can be shown to fail. To require correction as a normal operation rather than a crisis response. To restore restraint as the default posture of power. This book does not promise better leaders or perfect outcomes. It offers something more modest and more durable: a way to prevent systems from drifting beyond their purpose while still appearing to work.

If governance is to remain legitimate, it must be able to explain itself, correct itself, and limit itself. This book is an exploration of how that can be done—without ideology, without revolution, and without abandoning the constitutional architecture that already exists.

CHAPTER 1

The Inversion

Modern governance no longer operates from purpose to outcome. Instead of Meaning guiding Policy and Policy directing Flow, resources and enforcement increasingly move first, policy adapts second, and meaning is retroactively justified last. This inversion does not require malice. It emerges naturally when systems optimize for continuity rather than correction. The result is stability without alignment—processes that persist while drifting from their stated ends.

At its core, governance is supposed to answer a simple question: what condition in the real world is this action meant to change? Meaning is the articulation of that answer. Policy is the authority structure designed to pursue it. Flow is the execution—money, enforcement, incentives, and operational force applied over time. When these elements remain ordered, systems remain legible. When they invert, systems continue to function while becoming increasingly detached from their original purpose.

The inversion begins subtly. Budgets roll forward because stopping them would be disruptive. Authorities are extended because letting them expire would require explanation. Programs persist because they employ people, support contractors, and stabilize expectations. Over time, continuity becomes the implicit goal. Once that happens, purpose is no longer the driver of action—it becomes a justification layered on top of action that is already underway.

This is how Meaning becomes secondary. Instead of asking whether a policy is still necessary, institutions ask how to defend it. Instead of measuring whether outcomes justify authority, they measure whether procedures were followed. Compliance replaces effectiveness as the standard of success. The system no longer asks whether it should act, only whether it acted correctly according to its own rules.

Flow accelerates this process. Once money, enforcement, and incentives are moving, they create gravitational pull. Entire ecosystems form around continued operation: vendors, agencies, advocacy groups, reporting frameworks, and professional expertise tied to the program's existence. These structures are not inherently corrupt. They are rational responses to incentives. But they make reversal costly, and correction politically risky.

Policy then adapts to protect Flow. Authorities are broadened to accommodate new conditions rather than revisited to assess necessity. Exceptions are carved out to handle edge cases without reconsidering the core design. Temporary measures become permanent through serial extension. Each adaptation is defensible in isolation. Collectively, they entrench the inversion.

Meaning is addressed last, often in the form of narrative. When outcomes disappoint, explanations are produced instead of redesign. External factors are blamed. Metrics are redefined. Success is reframed. The original purpose is rarely revisited directly, because doing so would raise uncomfortable questions about whether the authority should continue to exist at all.

This inversion explains why systems can expand while trust declines. From the inside, institutions are busy, compliant, and procedurally correct. From the outside, results feel disconnected from promises. The gap between effort and outcome widens, not because people stop working, but because work is no longer oriented around a clearly bounded objective.

The critical point is that inversion is structural, not partisan. It appears under every ideology and administration. Conservative systems invert toward market stabilization without accountability. Progressive systems invert toward protection without measurement. Technocratic systems invert toward complexity without clarity. The form changes; the pattern does not.

A useful way to see the inversion is to examine the order in which questions are asked. In a coherent system, the sequence is:

What condition are we trying to change?

What authority is necessary—and no more than necessary—to pursue it?

What resources and enforcement are required, and for how long?

In an inverted system, the sequence becomes:

What resources and authorities already exist?

How do we adapt policy to keep them functioning?

What explanation best justifies continuation?

Once this reversal takes hold, correction becomes exceptional rather than routine. Failure no longer triggers redesign; it triggers expansion, modification, or narrative defense. The system grows more complex in response to its own shortcomings, which further obscures meaning and makes evaluation harder.

The inversion also weakens constitutional safeguards. Separation of powers presumes that authority is temporary and reviewable. When Flow dominates, review becomes symbolic. Oversight hearings occur, reports are issued, but little changes because the underlying motion of the system is never paused. Authority persists by default, rather than by renewed consent.

Importantly, this does not mean that outcomes are always negative. Inverted systems can produce real benefits, especially early on. The problem is not initial effectiveness but long-term drift. Without enforced reversion to neutrality—without moments where action stops and purpose is revalidated—systems accumulate contradictions. They do more while meaning less.

This is why crises become the primary mechanism for change. When correction is not built into normal operation, it only occurs when failure becomes undeniable. Emergency replaces governance as the reset function. After the crisis passes, the system stabilizes again—often larger, more complex, and more inverted than before.

The inversion is therefore self-reinforcing. Stability masks misalignment. Misalignment increases complexity. Complexity delays correction. Delay increases reliance on crisis. Crisis justifies further expansion. The cycle repeats.

This book begins with the inversion because it is the root condition. Without recognizing it, reform efforts treat symptoms rather than structure. They add new rules, new oversight bodies, new reporting requirements—all of which increase Flow without restoring Meaning. The result is reform that feels active but changes little.

To reverse the inversion, the order must be restored. Meaning must be explicit, measurable, and primary. Authority must be bounded, temporary, and reviewable. Flow must be traceable, constrained, and interruptible. Correction must be normal, not catastrophic.

The remaining chapters do not argue for what outcomes should be chosen. They focus on how decisions are structured so that outcomes—whatever they are—remain accountable to purpose. The task is not to perfect governance, but to make drift visible and correction unavoidable.

Only once the inversion is understood can alignment be restored.

Understood. Only Chapter 1. Nothing else.

CHAPTER 1 — The Inversion

Citations & Supporting Authority

Constitutional Text

U.S. Constitution, Article I, Section 8 — Powers must be affirmatively authorized.

U.S. Constitution, Article I, Section 9 — Explicit limits on governmental action.

Appropriations Clause — No expenditure without prior legislative authorization.

Supreme Court Precedent

Youngstown Sheet & Tube Co. v. Sawyer — Executive action cannot precede or substitute for authorization.

INS v. Chadha — Constitutional sequence cannot be bypassed for efficiency.

West Virginia v. EPA — Major Questions Doctrine: authority must be explicit before action.

Utility Air Regulatory Group v. EPA — Agencies may not redefine meaning to justify existing regulatory flow.

Statutory / Administrative Practice

Continuing Resolutions replacing outcome-based appropriations.

Serial renewal of emergency declarations without redefinition of necessity.

Broad delegations followed by expansive rulemaking and post-hoc justification.

Historical / Empirical Record

GAO findings of programs continuing without outcome-based review.

Persistent authority without enforced sunsets.

Budget growth decoupled from performance metrics.

Proof of Coherence — Chapter 1

Claim

Modern governance operates in inverted order: Flow → Policy → Meaning, rather than Meaning → Policy → Flow.

Falsifiability Condition

Documented evidence of routine, system-wide pause-before-action, where purpose is explicitly defined and bounded before authority and resources are deployed.

Supporting Authority

Appropriations Clause; separation-of-powers jurisprudence; Major Questions Doctrine.

Observed Pattern

Resources and enforcement are deployed first; statutory interpretation and narrative justification follow execution.

Status

Claim remains coherent. Falsifiability threshold not met.

CHAPTER 2

Recurrence Across Systems

Applying the inversion established in Chapter 1

The same inversion appears regardless of sector. Whether in economic regulation, emergency authority, infrastructure, or social policy, the pattern repeats: funds deploy before outcomes are defined, authority persists beyond necessity, and review occurs only after damage accumulates. The recurrence is not ideological. It is architectural.

What makes the inversion difficult to confront is not its visibility, but its familiarity. Once a pattern becomes standard practice across multiple domains, it no longer appears as a failure of design. It appears as "how things work." The repetition itself becomes justification. If every sector behaves the same way, the behavior is assumed to be inevitable rather than chosen.

Across systems, the sequence is consistent. First, a problem is identified, often under conditions of urgency or political pressure. Second, resources and authority are deployed quickly, sometimes appropriately, sometimes excessively. Third, the system stabilizes around that deployment. Only later—often much later—does anyone ask whether the original condition has changed, whether the authority is still necessary, or whether the outcomes justify continuation. By then, reversal is costly.

In economic regulation, the inversion manifests through persistent intervention untethered from measurable targets. Programs intended to stabilize markets or protect consumers often begin with a clear justification. Over time, however, the metrics that defined success fade, while the regulatory structures remain. Enforcement continues because the authority exists, not because the condition persists. Policy adapts to maintain enforcement capacity, and meaning shifts from solving a problem to managing a permanent regulatory environment.

Emergency authority provides one of the clearest examples of recurrence. Emergencies justify rapid action, suspended norms, and expanded discretion. In the moment, this is often necessary. The inversion occurs when emergency powers outlive the emergency itself. Instead of reversion to baseline, exceptions normalize. Extensions are granted not because conditions demand them, but because ending them would require admitting that authority is no longer needed. Review becomes symbolic, and renewal becomes routine.

Infrastructure systems invert through funding momentum. Large-scale projects require long timelines, complex coordination, and significant capital. Once funding is allocated and construction begins, continuation becomes the overriding goal. Cost overruns are tolerated because stopping would be worse. Delays are justified because progress is visible. Outcome definitions—what the infrastructure was supposed to enable—gradually disappear behind schedules, budgets, and technical milestones. Flow persists regardless of whether the original need still exists in the same form.

Social policy demonstrates the inversion through benefit persistence and expansion without outcome reconciliation. Programs designed to address specific social conditions often lack clear exit criteria. Success is measured by participation or spending rather than improvement in the underlying condition. When outcomes fail to improve, the response is rarely contraction or redesign. Instead, eligibility expands, funding increases, and administrative complexity grows. The system becomes a manager of conditions rather than a solver of them.

What unites these examples is not intent, but sequence. In each case, Flow establishes permanence. Policy adapts to preserve that permanence. Meaning becomes elastic—reinterpreted to fit what already exists. The system does not ask whether it should continue; it asks how to continue.

This recurrence also explains why oversight frequently fails. Oversight mechanisms are often procedural rather than structural. Hearings are held. Reports are issued. Findings are acknowledged. But unless Flow is paused or authority is bounded, oversight remains advisory. It observes motion without interrupting it. Review occurs after damage accumulates precisely because review lacks the power to force reversion.

The architectural nature of the inversion becomes clearer when comparing systems with vastly different goals. Economic markets, public health, national security, education, and environmental regulation share little ideologically. Yet the same governance behaviors emerge. This indicates that the cause is not belief, but structure. Systems reward continuity. They penalize interruption. They resist self-termination.

Once a system has inverted, even well-intentioned actors operate within its constraints. Officials inherit authorities they did not design. Budgets arrive pre-allocated. Programs exist with constituencies attached. Attempting correction requires political capital, administrative effort, and public explanation. Maintaining the status quo requires none. In such an environment, drift is not a failure of character; it is the path of least resistance.

The recurrence across systems also produces a false sense of inevitability. Because inversion is everywhere, it feels natural. Reform efforts often fail because they target surface features rather than the underlying order. They add new compliance requirements, create new oversight bodies, or introduce new metrics without changing the sequence in which decisions are made. Flow continues first. Everything else follows.

This is why reforms frequently increase complexity without improving outcomes. Each layer is added to correct the failures of the previous layer, but none address the inversion itself. Complexity becomes a substitute for alignment. The system appears more sophisticated while becoming less intelligible.

Another consequence of recurrence is fragmentation of responsibility. When systems are inverted, no single actor feels accountable for outcomes. Legislators fund programs but do not control execution. Executives execute programs but do not define meaning. Courts review disputes but cannot redesign structure. Each branch acts within its domain while the overall system drifts. Accountability diffuses until it disappears.

Importantly, recurrence does not imply that all systems are equally broken. Some perform better than others. Some are closer to alignment. But without structural correction, even effective systems accumulate drift over time. Success delays correction just as surely as failure, because success reduces pressure to re-examine authority.

The repetition across systems reveals the true scale of the problem. This is not a matter of fixing one agency, reforming one policy area, or electing different officials. It is a question of operating order. As long as Flow precedes Meaning, systems will stabilize before they align.

Recognizing recurrence is essential because it prevents false solutions. If the inversion were confined to one sector, targeted reform might suffice. But because it is architectural, correction must also be architectural. The order of decision-making must change everywhere it applies, or nowhere it does.

The chapters that follow move from diagnosis to design. Having established that the inversion repeats across systems, the next step is to examine the constitutional architecture that was meant to prevent it—and how that architecture can be restored without expanding power or abandoning democratic constraint.

The problem is not that governance is too weak.

It is that it no longer knows how to stop.

CHAPTER 2 — Recurrence Across Systems

Citations and Supporting Authority

Constitutional Text

U.S. Constitution, Article I — Requirement of legislative authorization and reauthorization.

U.S. Constitution, Article II — Execution limited to granted authority.

U.S. Constitution, Article III — Judicial review as post-action correction, not pre-authorization.

Federalist No. 47 and No. 51 — Structural separation to prevent accumulation of power through functional overlap.

Supreme Court Precedent

Youngstown Sheet & Tube Co. v. Sawyer — Emergency justification does not eliminate the requirement for proper sequence.

INS v. Chadha — Structural violations cannot be cured by convenience or widespread practice.

Brown v. Board of Education — Demonstrates delayed correction after prolonged systemic failure.

Free Enterprise Fund v. PCAOB — Accumulated insulation across systems undermines accountability.

West Virginia v. EPA — Reasserts that recurrence of practice does not legitimize unauthorized authority.

Statutory and Administrative Practice

Serial reauthorization of emergency powers without redefining triggering conditions.

Multi-sector reliance on continuing resolutions rather than outcome-based appropriations.

Delegation of broad regulatory authority across economic, health, environmental, and security domains.

Administrative rulemaking substituting for legislative reexamination.

Historical and Empirical Record

Government Accountability Office recurring "High Risk List" identifying the same agencies over decades.

Inspector General reports documenting unresolved findings repeated across review cycles.

CBO analyses showing program cost growth independent of outcome improvement.

Normalization of crisis-based governance across unrelated policy domains.

Proof of Coherence — Chapter 2

Claim

The inversion of Meaning, Policy, and Flow recurs across sectors because it is produced by governance architecture rather than ideology.

Falsifiability Condition

Evidence of sector-specific correction where systems independently restore pause-before-action, bounded authority, and outcome-based reauthorization without external intervention.

Supporting Authority

Separation of powers doctrine; repeated Supreme Court correction of structural accumulation; constitutional requirement of reauthorization and review.

Observed Pattern

Economic, emergency, infrastructure, and social systems all exhibit the same sequence: deployment precedes definition, authority persists, and review follows harm.

Status

Claim remains coherent. Cross-sector recurrence confirms architectural origin rather than ideological cause.

CHAPTER 3

Constitutional Architecture as a Trinary System

The Constitution encodes a three-part equilibrium: purpose, authority, and execution. These are distributed across equal branches, each primary in one function and constrained in the others. Stability emerges not from dominance, but from rotation—meaning is interpreted, authority is granted, flow is executed, and correction is perpetual.

At the founding, governance was not designed as a linear command structure. It was designed as a system that assumes error, anticipates drift, and embeds restraint as a permanent condition. The Constitution does not attempt to perfect decision-making; it attempts to prevent accumulation of unchecked power. To do this, it separates governance into distinct functions that must remain in tension. When those functions remain ordered, the system corrects itself. When they collapse into one another, inversion begins.

The three functions at the heart of constitutional design are meaning, authority, and execution. Meaning refers to the interpretation of purpose—what the law intends to accomplish and how it should be understood in context. Authority refers to the granting of permission—who may act, under what scope, and for how long. Execution refers to the application of force—money spent, rules enforced, and actions taken in the real world. Each function is essential. None is sufficient alone.

The legislative branch is primary in authority. Congress grants permission through statutes and appropriations. It defines the scope of action and controls duration through funding cycles, sunsets, and reauthorization. At the same time, Congress is constrained in execution. It does not administer programs or enforce laws. Its role is not to act directly, but to define the conditions under which action may occur.

When Congress attempts to execute policy rather than authorize it, it undermines its own legitimacy and disrupts the equilibrium.

The executive branch is primary in execution. It applies the law, deploys resources, and enforces rules. It translates permission into action. At the same time, the executive is constrained in meaning. It may interpret statutes only within the bounds set by law and subject to review. The executive does not own purpose; it inherits it. When executive discretion expands to redefine meaning rather than execute it, authority shifts without consent.

The judicial branch is primary in meaning. Courts interpret disputes, clarify boundaries, and ensure that authority and execution remain tethered to law. They do not initiate policy or administer programs. Their power lies in limitation, not action. When courts attempt to substitute their preferences for legislative purpose or executive execution, they disrupt the equilibrium in a different direction.

These roles are not hierarchical. Each branch is equal in legitimacy, but asymmetric in function. The system remains stable only if no branch permanently occupies another's primary domain. Rotation—not control—is the stabilizing mechanism. Authority is granted, execution follows, meaning is tested, and correction occurs through review and renewal. This rotation is the constitutional equivalent of feedback.

When this trinary structure functions properly, no branch needs to dominate. Congress does not need to micromanage execution because it controls permission and funding. The executive does not need to redefine law because it is bounded by statute. The judiciary does not need to govern because it can correct excess through interpretation. Power remains distributed because correction is continuous.

Inverted systems disrupt this rotation. Authority persists without renewal. Execution continues without pause. Meaning adapts to justify what already exists. When this happens, branches still appear separate, but their functional roles blur. Congress funds without redefining purpose. The executive executes without clear bounds. Courts review after the fact without structural remedies. The system moves, but no longer rotates.

This breakdown often masquerades as efficiency. Concentrated authority appears faster. Continuous execution appears productive. Deferred review appears pragmatic. But efficiency without rotation is instability delayed. The longer correction is postponed, the more disruptive it becomes when it finally occurs.

The Constitution anticipated this risk. That is why it embedded time into authority. Appropriations expire. Terms end. Laws can be repealed. Amendments require consensus. Nothing is meant to be permanent without renewal. Permanence is the enemy of correction.

The trinary structure also explains why neutrality matters. Each branch must default to restraint in the domains where it is not primary. Congress should not execute. The executive should not legislate. Courts should not administer. Neutrality is not inaction; it is role fidelity. When branches remain neutral outside their primary function, the system remains legible.

This framework reframes checks and balances not as opposition, but as alignment. The goal is not to block action, but to ensure that action remains tethered to purpose and consent. Checks exist not to create gridlock, but to force reconsideration. Balance exists not to weaken government, but to prevent irreversible error.

Understanding the Constitution as a trinary system clarifies why reform efforts often fail. Many reforms attempt to strengthen one branch at the expense of others. They add executive discretion to overcome legislative delay, judicial deference to speed regulation, or legislative micromanagement to control agencies. Each move addresses a symptom while worsening the underlying imbalance.

Restoration does not require empowering a single branch. It requires reestablishing rotation. Meaning must be clarified and tested. Authority must be bounded and renewed. Execution must be observable and interruptible. Correction must be normal, not exceptional.

This is why neutrality is central to coherence. The default state of the system is not action, but readiness. When a branch detects misalignment—ambiguous purpose, unbounded authority, or opaque execution—the correct response is not escalation, but reversion. Action pauses. Authority tightens. Meaning is reexamined. Only then can execution resume legitimately.

The Constitution does not promise that governance will always succeed. It promises that governance can always be corrected. The trinary structure is the mechanism that makes that promise credible.

When understood this way, the Constitution is not a static document. It is an operating system. Its stability does not come from rigidity, but from disciplined motion—movement constrained by role, time, and review. Power flows, but it must return.

The chapters that follow build on this architecture. Having identified the inversion and established the trinary equilibrium that was meant to prevent it, the next step is to define how neutrality, correction, and validation can be operationalized in modern systems without violating constitutional limits.

The Constitution already contains the answer.

The task is to use it as designed.

CHAPTER 3 — Constitutional Architecture as a Trinary System

Citations and References

Constitutional Text

U.S. Constitution, Article I — Legislative authority to grant permission, define scope, and set duration.

U.S. Constitution, Article II — Executive authority limited to execution of granted power.

U.S. Constitution, Article III — Judicial authority to interpret law and enforce constitutional limits.

Separation of Powers Doctrine — Functional division as a safeguard against accumulation.

Checks and Balances Framework — Mutual restraint through institutional design.

Federalist No. 47 — Concentration of legislative, executive, and judicial power constitutes tyranny.

Federalist No. 51 — Structural checks, not virtue, preserve liberty.

Supreme Court Precedent

Marbury v. Madison — Judicial review establishes meaning as a corrective function.

Buckley v. Valeo — Clear separation required between authorization and execution.

Bowsher v. Synar — Congress may not retain control over execution after delegating authority.

Morrison v. Olson — Balance depends on functional separation, not formal labels.

Seila Law LLC v. CFPB — Consolidation of authority undermines constitutional accountability.

Free Enterprise Fund v. PCAOB — Excessive insulation across branches erodes control and review.

Statutory and Administrative Practice

Independent agencies exercising rulemaking, enforcement, and adjudication within a single body.

Legislative oversight conducted without interrupting execution or funding.

Judicial remedies applied after harm rather than preventing unauthorized consolidation.

Delegated authority operating without effective temporal or scope limits.

Historical and Empirical Record

Expansion of the administrative state beyond original constitutional assumptions.

Repeated judicial intervention correcting post hoc consolidation of powers.

Decline of meaningful legislative reauthorization across federal programs.

Persistence of authority without enforced sunset or rotation.

Proof of Coherence — Chapter 3

Claim

The Constitution encodes a three-part equilibrium of meaning, authority, and execution distributed across equal branches, stabilized through rotation and restraint rather than dominance.

Falsifiability Condition

Demonstrated constitutional legitimacy for permanent consolidation of interpretive, authorizing, and executive power within a single branch or entity without corrective intervention.

Supporting Authority

Separation of powers doctrine; Supreme Court jurisprudence repeatedly invalidating consolidation; constitutional requirement of role distinction.

Observed Pattern

Judicial correction consistently occurs when branches or agencies collapse multiple functions into a single locus of control.

Status

Claim remains coherent. Constitutional practice confirms trinary equilibrium through corrective enforcement.

CHAPTER 4

The Neutral Baseline

The Constitution presumes restraint. Action is not the default; justification is. The Neutral Baseline represents the lawful state of rest—where no expansion occurs absent clear purpose, bounded authority, and review. All durable governance begins here.

Restraint is often misunderstood as inaction or weakness. In constitutional design, it is neither. Restraint is the condition that makes legitimate action possible. The Neutral Baseline is not a pause imposed by indecision; it is the default posture from which all authority must depart and to which it must be capable of returning. Without a baseline, there is no reference point. Without a reference point, drift cannot be detected.

At the founding, restraint was assumed because power was understood to be dangerous when left unchecked. The Constitution does not ask government to prove why it should act; it asks government to prove why it should continue acting. Authority is granted temporarily, conditionally, and subject to renewal. The Neutral Baseline exists to ensure that permission is never assumed by inertia.

In practical terms, the Neutral Baseline is the state in which no program expands automatically, no authority renews itself by default, and no resources continue to flow without periodic justification. It is the posture of "show cause." Why does this action still exist? What condition does it address today? What authority does it require now, not historically? These questions are not exceptional. They are routine.

Modern governance departs from this baseline almost immediately. Action becomes the norm. Programs are funded year over year. Authorities roll forward. Emergency measures persist. The system treats continuity as harmless and interruption as risky. Over time, restraint becomes framed as obstruction, even though restraint is the constitutional standard.

The loss of the Neutral Baseline explains why so many systems cannot stop. Once action is continuous, any attempt to pause appears disruptive. Workers depend on programs. Contractors depend on funding. Agencies depend on authority. Political actors depend on avoiding blame. The cost of stopping grows higher the longer restraint is deferred. As a result, restraint disappears not because it was rejected, but because it was postponed.

The Neutral Baseline is also where legitimacy is renewed. Consent is not a one-time event. It is an ongoing condition. When authority persists without reauthorization, consent becomes implied rather than explicit. The baseline forces consent back into view. It requires that authority be granted again, not merely extended.

This is why time is integral to restraint. The Constitution embeds time everywhere: elections, terms, appropriations, and review. Time is the mechanism that pulls systems back toward neutrality. When time limits are removed or bypassed, systems lose their natural return path. Authority becomes sticky. Flow becomes permanent. Correction becomes extraordinary.

Neutrality also protects against overreaction. In crisis conditions, rapid action may be necessary. The Neutral Baseline does not prevent emergency response; it ensures that emergency response does not become normal governance. Without a baseline to return to, exceptions accumulate. What began as a temporary deviation becomes a new standard. The baseline prevents exception from redefining the rule.

The Neutral Baseline is therefore inseparable from due process. Due process is not merely procedural fairness in individual cases. It is the systemic principle that power must justify itself before it acts and again before it continues acting. Neutrality is due process applied to governance itself.

Importantly, neutrality does not mean that no work occurs. Monitoring continues. Measurement continues. Evaluation continues. What stops is expansion without justification. The system remains attentive, not inert. In this sense, the Neutral Baseline is a state of readiness. It is governance holding its breath, not asleep.

This distinction matters because critics often frame restraint as paralysis. In reality, paralysis occurs when systems cannot correct themselves. Neutrality enables correction by making pause legitimate. When pause is legitimate, redesign is possible. When pause is illegitimate, systems compensate by layering complexity on top of failure.

The Neutral Baseline also clarifies accountability. When action must restart from justification, responsibility becomes visible. Who is requesting authority? For what purpose? For how long? Under what conditions will it end? These questions attach names, votes, and signatures to power. Without neutrality, accountability diffuses into process and paperwork.

One of the most damaging consequences of losing the Neutral Baseline is the normalization of "because it exists" as a justification. Programs continue because they exist. Authorities persist because they were granted once. Funds flow because they flowed last year. This logic is antithetical to constitutional design. Existence is not legitimacy.

Restoring the Neutral Baseline does not require dismantling government. It requires reasserting the presumption of restraint. It requires treating authority as borrowed, not owned. It requires making pause a normal operation rather than a political failure.

In a trinary system, neutrality is the center state. It is the point from which misalignment is detected and to which correction returns. Without a center, the system oscillates wildly or locks into permanent motion. Neutrality is the stabilizer.

This is why the Neutral Baseline is foundational to everything that follows. Correction cannot occur unless pause is legitimate. Validation cannot occur unless restraint precedes action. Alignment cannot persist unless systems can return to rest.

The Constitution does not ask government to be inactive. It asks government to be reversible. The Neutral Baseline is the condition that makes reversibility possible.

The chapters ahead build on this premise. Having established the inversion, the recurrence across systems, the trinary constitutional architecture, and the necessity of neutrality, the next step is to examine how misalignment is detected—and how systems can be designed to return to the baseline without crisis, blame, or collapse.

Durable governance does not rush forward.

It knows how to stop.

CHAPTER 4 — The Neutral Baseline

Citations and References

Constitutional Text

U.S. Constitution, Preamble — Government instituted to secure liberty through ordered authority.

U.S. Constitution, Article I, Section 8 — Authority must be affirmatively granted.

U.S. Constitution, Article I, Section 9 — Explicit prohibitions constrain action absent justification.

U.S. Constitution, Article II — Executive power limited to faithful execution of law.

Due Process Clauses (Fifth and Fourteenth Amendments) — Power must justify itself before action and continuation.

Supreme Court Precedent

Youngstown Sheet & Tube Co. v. Sawyer — Absence of authorization places executive action at its lowest ebb.

Hamdi v. Rumsfeld — Emergency does not eliminate due process or justify indefinite authority.

Boumediene v. Bush — Constitutional restraints persist even under exceptional conditions.

INS v. Chadha — Structural requirements enforce restraint even when inconvenient.

Statutory and Administrative Practice

Automatic renewal of authorities without reauthorization hearings.

Continuing resolutions maintaining funding without outcome review.

Emergency powers extended beyond triggering conditions.

Program continuation treated as default absent affirmative justification.

Historical and Empirical Record

Normalization of temporary measures into permanent governance tools.

GAO findings documenting lack of sunset enforcement across agencies.

Inspector General reports identifying continuation without reassessment.

Erosion of pause-and-review practices in federal administration.

Proof of Coherence — Chapter 4

Claim

The Constitution presumes restraint, establishing neutrality as the lawful baseline from which all authority must depart and to which it must be capable of returning.

Falsifiability Condition

Evidence that constitutional governance authorizes continuous expansion or renewal of authority without affirmative justification, time limits, or review.

Supporting Authority

Due process jurisprudence; separation of powers doctrine; repeated judicial rejection of indefinite or self-renewing authority.

Observed Pattern

Authorities and programs persist by default, with pause framed as exceptional rather than normal.

Status

Claim remains coherent. Constitutional practice affirms restraint as the baseline condition.

CHAPTER 5

Misalignment as Signal

Failure is not evidence of corruption; it is evidence of uncorrected drift. Misalignment is detectable when meaning becomes ambiguous, authority unbounded, or flow opaque. The error of modern systems is not failure—but the refusal to revert to neutrality when failure appears.

Chapter 5

Misalignment as Signal

Failure is not evidence of corruption; it is evidence of uncorrected drift. Misalignment is detectable when meaning becomes ambiguous, authority unbounded, or flow opaque. The error of modern systems is not failure—but the refusal to revert to neutrality when failure appears.

Modern governance treats failure as an anomaly—something to be explained away, denied, or managed politically. In reality, failure is a normal and necessary condition of any complex system. What determines whether a system remains healthy is not whether it fails, but whether it can recognize failure early and respond appropriately. Misalignment is the earliest detectable form of failure, and it appears long before collapse, scandal, or crisis.

Misalignment occurs when the relationship between purpose, authority, and execution loses coherence. Meaning drifts when objectives are no longer clearly stated, measurable, or relevant to current conditions. Authority drifts when powers persist without renewal, expand without constraint, or operate beyond their original scope. Flow drifts when resources move without transparency, concentrate without justification, or continue independently of outcomes. Any one of these conditions is sufficient to signal misalignment. Together, they indicate systemic drift.

The critical insight is that misalignment is not a moral judgment. It does not imply bad faith, incompetence, or conspiracy. It is a diagnostic state. Systems drift because they are designed to persist, not to stop. Without enforced return points, drift is the expected outcome. Treating misalignment as wrongdoing turns correction into punishment, which discourages early detection and honest reporting. Treating misalignment as signal turns correction into maintenance.

Most institutions lack a shared definition of failure. Instead, they substitute proxies: compliance rates, spending levels, program participation, or procedural milestones. These measures describe activity, not alignment. A system can be highly active and deeply misaligned. In fact, activity often increases as misalignment grows, because complexity rises to compensate for unresolved contradictions.

Ambiguous meaning is the first and most subtle signal. When a policy's purpose can no longer be stated plainly, when success cannot be distinguished from continuation, or when goals shift without formal acknowledgment, meaning has drifted. This often appears as mission creep, vague language, or constantly revised objectives. Ambiguity allows authority to persist without accountability because no one can agree on what success would look like.

Unbounded authority is the second signal. Authority drifts when it lacks time limits, renewal requirements, or scope constraints. Temporary measures become permanent. Discretion expands to handle exceptions. Review becomes perfunctory. Authority that is not periodically re-justified becomes self-legitimating. At that point, the question is no longer whether authority is still needed, but how it should be exercised.

Opaque flow is the third signal. Flow becomes misaligned when money, enforcement, or incentives move without clear linkage to purpose. This includes spending that cannot be traced to outcomes, enforcement actions detached from original intent, or resource concentrations that persist regardless of performance. Opacity does not require secrecy. Complexity alone can obscure flow sufficiently to prevent meaningful review.

These signals often appear independently, but they reinforce one another. Ambiguous meaning makes authority harder to bound. Unbounded authority makes flow harder to interrupt. Opaque flow makes outcomes harder to evaluate. Together, they create a system that continues to operate while becoming increasingly resistant to correction.

The traditional response to failure is escalation. When outcomes disappoint, systems add new layers: additional funding, expanded authority, revised rules, or new oversight bodies. Escalation assumes that failure results from insufficient action rather than misordered action. In an inverted system, escalation accelerates drift by increasing flow before restoring meaning or bounding authority.

A coherent system responds differently. When misalignment is detected, the response is not escalation but reversion. Action pauses. Expansion stops. Authority tightens. Purpose is restated. This return to the Neutral Baseline is not retreat; it is recalibration. It creates the conditions under which correction can occur without compounding error.

The refusal to revert to neutrality is the defining error of modern systems. Pause is framed as weakness. Admission of failure is framed as liability. Correction is deferred in favor of continuity. Over time, the system loses the ability to distinguish between persistence and success. Everything that continues is treated as justified.

This refusal also distorts accountability. When systems cannot pause, individuals become scapegoats. Blame replaces diagnosis. Political narratives substitute for structural repair. The underlying design remains untouched, guaranteeing recurrence. Treating misalignment as signal avoids this cycle by shifting focus from fault to function.

Importantly, misalignment does not always produce immediate harm. Some systems deliver benefits even while drifting. This makes early signals easy to ignore. Success masks structural weakness. But drift accumulates. Over time, the cost of correction rises while the capacity to correct diminishes. Eventually, only crisis can force change.

Crisis-driven correction is the most destructive form of governance. It concentrates power, suspends norms, and accelerates flow under extreme conditions. While crises can reset systems, they do so at high social, economic, and institutional cost. A system that relies on crisis to correct itself is inherently unstable.

Detecting misalignment early requires explicit thresholds. Meaning must be testable. Authority must have expiration. Flow must be traceable. Without thresholds, misalignment remains subjective and politically contested. With thresholds, misalignment becomes a shared, observable condition that triggers predetermined response.

This is why misalignment must be treated as a state, not an accusation. A system can enter misalignment without anyone doing anything wrong. What matters is whether the system has a lawful path back to neutrality. If it does, correction can occur calmly and routinely. If it does not, misalignment hardens into failure.

Reversion to neutrality restores optionality. It reopens design space. It allows authority to be reconsidered, policies to be redesigned, and resources to be reallocated based on current conditions rather than historical momentum. Without reversion, systems are trapped by their past decisions.

Misalignment, properly understood, is a gift. It is early warning. It tells the system where it has drifted before damage becomes irreversible. Ignoring that signal is not strength. It is denial.

The chapters that follow build on this understanding. Having established neutrality as the baseline and misalignment as signal, the next task is to define how systems can revert lawfully, predictably, and without blame—and how validation can occur only after correction has been verified.

Failure does not destroy systems.

Refusal to listen does.

CHAPTER 5 — Misalignment as Signal

Citations and References

Constitutional Text

U.S. Constitution, Article I — Authority conditioned on scope, duration, and purpose.

U.S. Constitution, Article II — Execution constrained by lawful authorization.

U.S. Constitution, Article III — Judicial review as a corrective mechanism after misalignment.

Fifth Amendment — Due process as a constraint on arbitrary or unjustified action.

Fourteenth Amendment — Equal protection and due process as safeguards against systemic drift.

Supreme Court Precedent

Youngstown Sheet & Tube Co. v. Sawyer — Misalignment occurs when execution exceeds authorization.

Motor Vehicle Manufacturers Association v. State Farm — Agencies must provide reasoned explanation when outcomes diverge from purpose.

FCC v. Fox Television Stations — Arbitrary shifts in meaning without justification violate due process.

Department of Homeland Security v. Regents of the University of California — Failure to acknowledge and address reliance interests signals misalignment.

West Virginia v. EPA — Structural misalignment requires explicit corrective authorization.

Statutory and Administrative Practice

Agencies altering policy rationale without revisiting statutory authority.

Expansion of discretionary enforcement beyond original legislative intent.

Program continuation despite documented outcome failure.

Reliance on procedural compliance in place of substantive alignment.

Historical and Empirical Record

GAO reports identifying persistent mission creep across agencies.

Inspector General findings documenting unresolved deficiencies across audit cycles.

CBO variance analyses showing divergence between projected and actual outcomes.

Longitudinal evidence of program persistence despite declining effectiveness.

Proof of Coherence — Chapter 5

Claim

Failure is an early signal of misalignment between meaning, authority, and flow, not evidence of corruption.

Falsifiability Condition

Evidence that systems routinely identify outcome failure and lawfully revert to neutrality without escalation, narrative defense, or authority expansion.

Supporting Authority

Administrative law requirements for reasoned decision-making; constitutional limits on arbitrary action; separation of powers correction mechanisms.

Observed Pattern

Outcome failure is met with expansion, reinterpretation, or procedural defense rather than pause and redesign.

Status

Claim remains coherent. Institutional behavior treats failure as something to manage rather than a signal to correct.

CHAPTER 6

Reversion and Correction

No system may move directly from failure to validation. All misaligned action must first return to neutrality, where authority is constrained and purpose clarified. Only after correction and verification may validation occur. This sequence—−1 → 0 → +1—is the core stabilizer.

Reversion is the most misunderstood operation in governance. It is often treated as retreat, surrender, or admission of incompetence. In reality, reversion is the mechanism that makes learning possible. Without reversion, systems can only escalate, defend, or collapse. Correction requires a lawful pause, and that pause must be legitimate rather than forced by crisis.

In an aligned system, reversion is routine. When misalignment is detected, expansion stops automatically. No new authorities are granted. No additional resources are deployed. Existing action continues only insofar as it is necessary to prevent harm, but discretionary growth is suspended. This creates a stable environment in which redesign can occur without compounding error.

Reversion is not punishment. It is a return to the Neutral Baseline. Authority is not revoked; it is constrained. Flow is not eliminated; it is made interruptible. Meaning is not abandoned; it is clarified. The system does not shut down. It recalibrates.

The refusal to revert is what turns manageable drift into systemic failure. When systems continue operating at full momentum despite evidence of misalignment, they lose the ability to distinguish between action and effectiveness. Correction becomes politically dangerous because it threatens continuity. As a result, systems double down on the very behaviors that produced failure.

Correction begins only after reversion has occurred. Correction is the deliberate redesign of policy, authority, or execution to restore coherence. It is not improvisation. It is structured adjustment guided by explicit criteria. Correction answers three questions: What was the intended purpose? What authority is truly necessary to pursue it? What form of execution best serves that purpose now?

Correction must be bounded in time. Open-ended correction is indistinguishable from delay. If redesign can occur indefinitely, reversion becomes paralysis. For correction to work, it must operate within a defined window. The purpose of that window is not speed, but discipline. Time pressure forces clarity.

Verification separates correction from assertion. A system does not become aligned because it claims to be corrected. It becomes aligned because outcomes change in measurable ways. Verification requires independent observation. It requires that metrics defined at the outset are evaluated honestly after correction is implemented. Without verification, validation is meaningless.

The temptation to skip reversion is strong. Systems want to move directly from failure to validation. They want to declare improvement without stopping. This is how narratives replace correction. The $-1 \rightarrow +1$ shortcut is the hallmark of inverted governance. It preserves flow while bypassing accountability.

The trinary sequence prevents this shortcut. The requirement to pass through neutrality enforces humility. It acknowledges that action itself may be part of the problem. It creates space to reconsider assumptions that would otherwise remain implicit. Most importantly, it makes reversal possible without collapse.

Reversion also protects against overcorrection. When systems attempt to fix failure without pausing, they often swing too far in the opposite direction. Authority is stripped too broadly. Resources are withdrawn too abruptly. New rules are imposed without testing. Neutrality provides a buffer. It allows incremental redesign rather than reactive overhaul.

Correction is most effective when it is narrow. Not every component of a system needs to change. Often, misalignment arises from a small number of structural flaws: an authority that outlived its purpose, a metric that no longer reflects reality, or a flow that became detached from outcomes. Reversion isolates these flaws by stripping away momentum.

The absence of formal reversion mechanisms explains why many systems rely on informal workarounds. Agencies issue guidance instead of revising rules. Legislatures hold hearings instead of rewriting statutes. Courts narrow interpretation instead of forcing redesign. These actions mitigate harm without restoring coherence. They are compensations, not corrections.

Reversion must be automatic, not discretionary. If reversion depends on political will, it will occur only when failure becomes undeniable. Automatic reversion—triggered by predefined thresholds—normalizes correction. It removes stigma. It treats misalignment as expected rather than exceptional.

Validation is the final step in the sequence, and it is provisional by design. Validation does not certify perfection. It confirms that a system has returned to coherence under current conditions. Authority remains bounded. Flow remains traceable. Meaning remains explicit. Validation lasts only as long as those conditions hold.

This provisional nature is essential. Systems evolve. Conditions change. What works today may drift tomorrow. Validation without expiration recreates the very permanence that caused inversion. Every validated action must remain subject to reversion if misalignment reappears.

The $-1 \rightarrow 0 \rightarrow +1$ sequence mirrors how healthy systems function outside governance. Engineering systems shut down before repair. Scientific hypotheses are falsified before acceptance. Financial controls halt transactions before reconciliation. Governance is the only domain where systems are expected to correct themselves while running at full speed.

Reversion restores symmetry between action and accountability. It ensures that the cost of stopping is lower than the cost of failing. When stopping is legitimate, correction is feasible. When stopping is taboo, systems become brittle.

One of the greatest advantages of formal reversion is that it reduces the need for blame. When reversion is procedural, no individual must be singled out for failure. The system itself acknowledges drift and corrects. This preserves institutional trust and encourages honest reporting.

Correction also benefits from transparency. When reversion occurs openly, the public can see that failure leads to redesign rather than denial. Trust does not require constant success. It requires visible learning. Systems that correct publicly may appear less confident in the short term, but they are more durable in the long term.

The stabilizing power of the trinary sequence lies in its simplicity. Misalignment triggers reversion. Reversion enables correction. Correction requires verification. Verification permits validation. No step can be skipped without undermining the whole.

This sequence is not a suggestion. It is a constraint. It limits how quickly systems can move forward, but it prevents them from drifting irreversibly. It replaces crisis-driven change with continuous adjustment.

The chapters ahead extend this sequence into practice. Having established the necessity of reversion and correction, the next step is to define how coherence can be measured, how thresholds can be set, and how systems can be evaluated without politicizing failure.

Progress that cannot pause is not progress.

It is momentum without direction.

CHAPTER 6 — Reversion and Correction

Citations and References

Constitutional Text

U.S. Constitution, Article I — Authority must be affirmatively granted and may be withdrawn or allowed to expire.

U.S. Constitution, Article I, Section 9 — Limits on governmental power and expenditure enforce reversibility.

U.S. Constitution, Article II — Executive duty is faithful execution, not self-expansion or self-correction.

U.S. Constitution, Article III — Judicial authority to invalidate action that exceeds lawful bounds.

Fifth Amendment — Due process requires lawful pause and justification before continuation of power.

Supreme Court Precedent

Youngstown Sheet & Tube Co. v. Sawyer — Executive action at its lowest ebb when authority is absent or exceeded.

INS v. Chadha — Structural correction required when constitutional sequence is bypassed.

Motor Vehicle Manufacturers Association v. State Farm — Agencies must pause and reconsider when prior reasoning fails.

Department of Homeland Security v. Regents of the University of California — Failure to properly reverse course without reasoned analysis violates administrative law.

Free Enterprise Fund v. PCAOB — Lack of effective control prevents lawful correction.

Statutory and Administrative Practice

Absence of automatic pause mechanisms when programs fail to meet stated objectives.

Correction attempts made through guidance or reinterpretation rather than authority reset.

Escalation of authority following failure rather than reversion to baseline.

Lack of enforced sunsets tied to outcome variance.

Historical and Empirical Record

GAO documentation of repeated corrective recommendations without implementation.

Inspector General reports showing unresolved findings persisting across review cycles.

Historical reliance on crisis to force authority reset rather than routine correction.

Pattern of post-failure expansion rather than contraction.

Proof of Coherence — Chapter 6

Claim

Misaligned systems must revert to neutrality before correction and validation can lawfully occur.

Falsifiability Condition

Evidence that systems routinely correct failure while maintaining full authority and uninterrupted execution without accumulating further misalignment.

Supporting Authority

Separation of powers doctrine; administrative law requirements for reasoned reconsideration; constitutional limits on indefinite authority.

Observed Pattern

Correction is attempted without pause, leading to escalation, narrative defense, or further drift.

Status

Claim remains coherent. Reversion is consistently absent in modern corrective practice.

Canonical Coherence Traversal

A Formal Walkthrough of Alignment Under Law

This section demonstrates how the framework operates end-to-end when instantiated in a real governance context. It is not an example, but a canonical traversal. Any system claiming coherence under law must be able to pass through these states in sequence.

State –1: Misalignment Detected

A system enters misalignment when one or more of the following conditions are observable:

Meaning becomes ambiguous, unfalsifiable, or retroactively defined.

Authority exceeds its original scope, duration, or justification.

Flow persists independently of outcomes or verification.

At this stage, the system is not illegitimate, but it is incoherent. Continued execution under these conditions increases drift. The presence of misalignment does not imply wrongdoing; it signals structural contradiction.

Trigger Condition

Misalignment is triggered when variance between intended outcome and observed result exceeds predefined tolerance, or when authority persists beyond its authorization without renewal.

This trigger is objective. It does not rely on motive, intent, or narrative framing.

Required Transition: Reversion to Neutrality (0)

Upon trigger, the system must revert to the Neutral Baseline.

Reversion consists of four mandatory actions:

Expansion pauses. No new authority or flow is introduced.

Existing authority is constrained to minimum harm-prevention functions.

Original meaning is restated explicitly, or formally revised.

Review cadence is activated under predefined timelines.

Reversion is not rollback. It is lawful suspension of escalation to restore legibility.

If reversion does not occur, the system cannot proceed to correction without compounding error.

State 0: Neutral Baseline

At neutrality, the system is neither failing nor validated. It is reset to a lawful state of rest.

In this state:

Authority exists only insofar as it is necessary to maintain continuity.

Flow is traceable, interruptible, and bounded.

Meaning is explicit, testable, and current.

Neutrality restores optionality. Redesign is now possible without crisis or blame.

Correction Phase

Correction occurs only from neutrality.

Correction answers three questions:

What condition is the system meant to address now?

What authority is necessary—and no more than necessary—to address it?

What execution best serves that purpose under current conditions?

Correction is time-bounded. Open-ended correction collapses back into drift.

Verification

After correction is implemented, outcomes are measured against the stated meaning using predefined metrics.

Verification is independent of intent. It evaluates results, not explanations.

If verification fails, the system remains at neutrality or reverts again. There is no shortcut.

State +1: Validated Alignment

Validation occurs only after successful verification.

In this state:

Authority is explicitly bounded and time-limited.

Flow is demonstrably linked to outcomes.

Meaning remains measurable and falsifiable.

Validation is provisional. It expires automatically upon:

Threshold breach,

Authority expiration,

Or change in underlying conditions.

Failure Mode (Skipped Neutrality)

If a system moves directly from misalignment (−1) to validation claims (+1) without passing through neutrality (0), the result is false coherence.

This produces:

Narrative justification,

Authority escalation,

And legitimacy erosion.

Such systems appear stable but are structurally unsound.

Summary Sequence

Misalignment (−1)

→ Reversion to Neutrality (0)

→ Correction

→ Verification

→ Provisional Validation (+1)

No step may be skipped without invalidating the outcome.

This traversal is the minimum viable path for coherence under law.

CHAPTER 7

Proof of Coherence

A system is coherent if it can be proven wrong. Meaning must be measurable, authority bounded, flow traceable, and correction executable. When variance exceeds tolerance, correction must occur within defined time limits. Coherence is not belief; it is behavior under constraint.

A system is coherent if it can be proven wrong. Meaning must be measurable, authority bounded, flow traceable, and correction executable. When variance exceeds tolerance, alignment must be reassessed rather than defended.

Most governance frameworks fail because they cannot be falsified. They rely on intentions, narratives, or procedural compliance rather than testable claims. As long as a system can explain itself, it is assumed to be working. Coherence demands a higher standard. A coherent system must expose the conditions under which it is no longer justified to continue.

Proof of coherence does not mean proving that outcomes are good. It means proving that outcomes are connected to purpose through lawful authority and observable action. A system that cannot demonstrate this connection is operating on assertion rather than evidence. Over time, assertion replaces accountability, and drift becomes invisible.

Meaning is the first test. A policy's purpose must be stated in terms that allow failure to be detected. Vague aspirations cannot be evaluated. If success cannot be distinguished from continuation, the system is incoherent by design. Meaning must specify what condition is expected to change, over what period, and within what tolerance. Without this, no amount of measurement can restore alignment.

Authority is the second test. Power must be bounded in scope, duration, and review. Authority that persists without renewal cannot be falsified, because there is no condition under which it is required to stop. Bounded authority creates a decision point. It forces a choice: reauthorize based on evidence, redesign based on failure, or allow authority to expire. Without this choice, coherence collapses into permanence.

Flow is the third test. Resources, enforcement, and incentives must be traceable from authorization to outcome. If flow cannot be observed, alignment cannot be evaluated. Opaque flow allows systems to appear active while outcomes stagnate. Traceability does not require perfect transparency; it requires sufficient visibility to link action to effect. Where that link is absent, coherence cannot be claimed.

Correction is the fourth test. A system that detects failure but cannot correct it is not coherent. Detection without correction produces paralysis or denial. Correction must be executable within defined limits. It must be possible to pause, redesign, and restart without dismantling the system or triggering crisis. If correction requires extraordinary intervention, coherence exists only in theory.

Together, these four conditions form a closed test loop. Meaning defines what to measure. Authority defines when to stop. Flow defines what is happening. Correction defines what to do when alignment fails. If any element is missing, the loop breaks.

Variance is the quantitative expression of misalignment. It measures the distance between intended outcomes and observed results. Variance does not imply wrongdoing. It implies deviation. Every complex system produces variance. The question is not whether variance exists, but how the system responds when variance exceeds tolerance.

Tolerance must be defined in advance. A system that decides after the fact how much failure is acceptable is not falsifiable. Predefined tolerance transforms disagreement into diagnosis. When variance crosses the threshold, the response is automatic. Debate may continue, but action changes regardless of opinion.

This is the point at which most systems fail. Instead of responding to variance, they reinterpret meaning. Metrics are adjusted. Time horizons are extended. External factors are emphasized. The system preserves itself by redefining success. Proof of coherence forbids this maneuver. Meaning is fixed at the point of authorization and may be revised only through formal correction, not narrative adjustment.

Independent verification is essential. Self-certification undermines falsifiability. A system cannot be both judge and subject of its own coherence. Verification does not require hostility; it requires separation. Independent review ensures that claims of alignment are tested against observable reality rather than internal consensus.

Coherence is not a static condition. It exists across time. A system may be coherent today and incoherent tomorrow. This is why proof must be continuous rather than episodic. Regular measurement, scheduled review, and automatic reversion maintain coherence as conditions change.

Importantly, proof of coherence does not eliminate disagreement. It relocates disagreement. Instead of arguing about intentions or narratives, debate focuses on thresholds, measurements, and corrective design. This shifts conflict from ideology to structure. It makes governance legible even when consensus is absent.

Proof of coherence also protects innovation. Systems that can be falsified can be improved. When failure is detectable and correctable, experimentation becomes safer. Authority can be granted temporarily. Flow can be tested in limited scope. Successful designs can be validated; unsuccessful ones can be abandoned without stigma.

The absence of proof produces the opposite effect. When systems cannot be falsified, innovation becomes risky because failure threatens legitimacy. As a result, systems stagnate. They defend existing designs rather than test alternatives. Coherence restores optionality by separating failure from collapse.

The trinary sequence—misalignment, neutrality, validation—depends on proof. Without measurable variance, there is no trigger. Without bounded authority, there is no pause. Without traceable flow, there is no diagnosis. Without executable correction, there is no recovery. Proof binds these elements into a single discipline.

This chapter establishes that coherence is not philosophical. It is operational. It is the capacity of a system to admit error, pause lawfully, redesign intelligently, and resume action with evidence. Any system that cannot do this will drift, regardless of intent.

The chapter that follows moves from proof to rhythm. Having defined how coherence is measured, the next task is to define how often systems must prove themselves—and how cadence replaces crisis as the primary mechanism of change.

Truth in governance is not belief.

It is reversibility under constraint.

CHAPTER 7 — Proof of Coherence

Citations and References

Constitutional Text

U.S. Constitution, Article I — Authority conditioned on clear grants and renewal.

U.S. Constitution, Article II — Execution limited to lawful scope and purpose.

U.S. Constitution, Article III — Judicial review as falsification mechanism.

Appropriations Clause — Flow contingent on authorization and accountability.

Fifth Amendment — Due process requires reasoned justification and reversibility.

Supreme Court Precedent

Motor Vehicle Manufacturers Association v. State Farm — Action must be supported by reasoned explanation; failure exposes incoherence.

FCC v. Fox Television Stations — Shifts in meaning require justification; arbitrary change violates due process.

Department of Homeland Security v. Regents of the University of California — Failure to confront contrary evidence invalidates action.

Whitman v. American Trucking Associations — Meaning must be intelligible; unfalsifiable standards are unlawful.

West Virginia v. EPA — Claims of authority must be explicit and testable; post-hoc rationalization is insufficient.

Statutory and Administrative Practice

Performance metrics selected after execution rather than at authorization.

Moving goalposts through revised guidance instead of formal correction.

Self-certification of success without independent verification.

Lack of predefined tolerance thresholds triggering pause or redesign.

Historical and Empirical Record

GAO critiques of programs lacking measurable objectives.

Inspector General findings citing unverifiable success claims.

CBO analyses showing divergence between projected and actual outcomes without corrective reset.

Judicial invalidation following prolonged reliance on unfalsifiable standards.

Proof of Coherence — Chapter 7

Claim

A system is coherent only if it can be proven wrong through measurable meaning, bounded authority, traceable flow, and executable correction.

Falsifiability Condition

Evidence that systems routinely accept disconfirming results and lawfully pause, redesign, and resume action without narrative redefinition of success.

Supporting Authority

Administrative law requirements for reasoned decision-making; constitutional due process; separation of powers enforcement.

Observed Pattern

Systems redefine metrics or extend timelines when results diverge, avoiding falsification.

Status

Claim remains coherent. Falsifiability is consistently resisted rather than operationalized.

CHAPTER 8

Governance Cadence

Stability depends on rhythm, not force. Measurement, review, and reauthorization must occur on predictable cycles. Cadence replaces crisis. Correction replaces accumulation.

Most governance systems do not fail because they lack authority. They fail because they lack timing. Decisions are made reactively, reviews are triggered by scandal or emergency, and correction occurs only after damage has compounded. In such systems, crisis becomes the organizing principle. Cadence—the regular, predictable rhythm of evaluation and renewal—is absent. Without cadence, restraint erodes and correction becomes traumatic.

Cadence is the temporal structure of governance. It determines when meaning is revisited, when authority expires, and when execution is evaluated. A system with cadence does not wait for outrage or collapse to assess itself. It schedules reassessment as a normal operation. This transforms review from a political event into an administrative function.

The Constitution embeds cadence deliberately. Elections recur. Terms end. Appropriations expire. Laws can be repealed. These temporal constraints were not meant to be inconveniences. They were meant to force reconsideration. Time is the lever that pulls power back toward neutrality. When cadence is respected, authority cannot outrun consent.

Modern governance weakens cadence by smoothing it out. Temporary measures are extended routinely. Emergency authorities are renewed automatically. Programs are reauthorized without reexamination. Review becomes ceremonial rather than consequential. The system continues to move, but its rhythm flattens. Without peaks and pauses, drift accumulates unnoticed.

Predictable cycles change incentives. When review is scheduled and unavoidable, systems prepare for it. Data is gathered. Outcomes are tracked. Assumptions are documented. When review is ad hoc, systems prepare narratives instead. They respond defensively rather than diagnostically. Cadence makes honesty rational.

Measurement is the first component of cadence. Metrics must be collected continuously, not assembled retrospectively. Measurement aligned to meaning allows variance to be detected early. When metrics are tied to review cycles, they become actionable rather than ornamental. Measurement without cadence produces reports. Measurement with cadence produces decisions.

Review is the second component. Review must be empowered to interrupt flow. A review that cannot pause authority or redirect resources is informational only. Effective review asks not whether procedures were followed, but whether purpose is being served. It evaluates alignment, not activity.

Reauthorization is the third component. Authority that must be renewed cannot become permanent by inertia. Reauthorization forces a choice: continue, redesign, or end. Each option is legitimate. What is illegitimate is avoidance. When reauthorization is automatic, cadence collapses into continuity.

Cadence also disciplines scope. Short cycles favor narrow authority. Broad, indefinite authority resists review because it cannot be meaningfully evaluated within a reasonable period. By aligning scope with review frequency, cadence prevents overreach. Authority that cannot be reviewed should not be granted.

One of the most damaging myths in governance is that frequent review slows progress. In reality, the opposite is true. Systems without cadence accumulate unresolved contradictions that eventually require massive intervention. Systems with cadence correct continuously, avoiding the buildup that leads to crisis.

Crisis-driven governance is governance without rhythm. It concentrates power abruptly, suspends normal processes, and accelerates flow under extreme conditions. While sometimes unavoidable, crisis correction is blunt and destabilizing. Cadence reduces reliance on crisis by making correction routine.

Cadence also redistributes accountability. When review is predictable, responsibility cannot be evaded. Actors know when their decisions will be examined. This discourages short-term optimization at the expense of long-term alignment. It aligns incentives with durability rather than immediacy.

Importantly, cadence does not require constant change. It requires constant readiness to change. Many systems will pass review unchanged. That outcome is not failure. It is confirmation. Cadence validates stability when stability is deserved.

The absence of cadence explains why systems become brittle. When authority persists unchecked, even small corrections feel threatening. The system resists adjustment because adjustment has been deferred too long. Cadence prevents this brittleness by keeping systems flexible.

Cadence also supports pluralism. In a divided society, consensus on outcomes may be rare. Cadence allows disagreement to persist without paralysis. Even when actors disagree on goals, they can agree on timing. Regular review provides a shared procedural rhythm that stabilizes conflict.

Designing cadence requires discipline. Review cycles must be frequent enough to detect drift, but not so frequent that redesign becomes constant. The appropriate interval depends on the system's scope and impact. What matters is that the interval is known in advance and cannot be bypassed without explicit justification.

When cadence is restored, governance regains its capacity to learn. Measurement informs review. Review triggers correction. Correction leads to reauthorization. The system moves forward, but it breathes.

This is the alternative to accumulation. Instead of layering new authority on top of unresolved failure, cadence clears space for redesign. Instead of waiting for collapse, it normalizes recalibration.

The next chapter brings the framework to its conclusion. Having established inversion, recurrence, architecture, neutrality, misalignment, correction, proof, and cadence, the final task is to show how restoration can occur without upheaval—how coherence can be rebuilt within existing institutions, using existing authority, by changing order rather than ideology.

Governance does not need to be louder.

It needs to keep time.

CHAPTER 8 — Governance Cadence

Citations and References

Constitutional Text

U.S. Constitution, Article I, Section 8 — Legislative authority granted on a temporal basis.

U.S. Constitution, Article I, Section 9 — Limits on duration and expenditure enforce periodic review.

U.S. Constitution, Article II — Executive authority exercised within time-bound permission.

U.S. Constitution, Article III — Judicial review operates after action, reinforcing the need for regular legislative cadence.

Elections and Term Limits — Embedded temporal mechanisms forcing renewal and reconsideration.

Supreme Court Precedent

INS v. Chadha — Constitutional structure requires repeated, formal reconsideration of authority.

Clinton v. City of New York — Executive alteration of legislatively timed processes violates constitutional order.

Free Enterprise Fund v. PCAOB — Excessive insulation disrupts regular accountability cycles.

Seila Law LLC v. CFPB — Removal restrictions interfering with cadence undermine democratic control.

West Virginia v. EPA — Long-standing practice does not excuse absence of explicit, renewed authorization.

Statutory and Administrative Practice

Continuing resolutions replacing regular appropriations cycles.

Automatic renewal of emergency authorities without reassessment of conditions.

Multi-year delegations without intermediate review requirements.

Performance reviews conducted irregularly or post-crisis rather than on schedule.

Historical and Empirical Record

GAO identification of programs remaining on "High Risk" lists for decades.

Inspector General reports showing repeated findings without resolution across review cycles.

CBO documentation of long-term spending growth absent periodic outcome validation.

Historical reliance on crises to force reassessment rather than routine review.

Proof of Coherence — Chapter 8

Claim

Governance stability depends on predictable cadence of measurement, review, and reauthorization rather than continuous force or crisis response.

Falsifiability Condition

Evidence that systems lacking regular review cycles maintain long-term alignment, accountability, and correction without accumulating unresolved drift.

Supporting Authority

Constitutional embedding of time limits; separation of powers doctrine; judicial rejection of insulated or self-renewing authority.

Observed Pattern

Absence of cadence leads to accumulation, brittleness, and crisis-driven correction rather than continuous adjustment.

Status

Claim remains coherent. Empirical and constitutional records confirm cadence as a stabilizing requirement.

CHAPTER 9

Restoration Without Revolution

This framework does not require constitutional amendment, institutional replacement, or ideological consensus. It restores what already exists: bounded authority, accountable execution, and measurable outcomes. The Constitution is sufficient. The discipline was lost.

Calls for reform often assume that the system itself is broken beyond repair. They propose sweeping structural changes, new institutions, or radical redistributions of power. While these approaches promise renewal, they frequently create instability without resolving the underlying problem. The failure addressed in this book is not constitutional inadequacy, but constitutional neglect. The architecture remains intact. What has eroded is adherence to its operating discipline.

Restoration begins by rejecting the false choice between stagnation and upheaval. Governance does not need to be reinvented to be corrected. It needs to be reordered. The principles required for alignment—restraint, rotation, review, and reversibility—are already embedded in existing institutions. What is missing is the consistent application of those principles as a system rather than as isolated practices.

The appeal of revolution lies in its clarity. It promises decisive action, moral resolution, and a clean break from failure. In practice, revolutions concentrate power temporarily and depend on exceptional authority to succeed. They often suspend the very constraints they claim to restore. Even when motivated by legitimate grievances, they risk replacing one form of drift with another. Restoration avoids this trap by working within constraint rather than escaping it.

The framework presented here operates entirely inside constitutional boundaries. It does not expand executive discretion, weaken legislative authority, or bypass judicial review. Instead, it clarifies roles and restores rotation. Congress regains primacy over authorization and duration. The executive executes within clear bounds. The judiciary enforces meaning through limitation rather than substitution. Each branch does less—but does it more precisely.

One of the most important aspects of restoration is normalization. Correction must become routine rather than exceptional. When reversion to neutrality is treated as failure, systems resist it. When reversion is treated as maintenance, systems adapt. Restoration reframes pause, redesign, and expiration as signs of health rather than weakness.

This approach also lowers the political cost of honesty. In a system without routine correction, admitting failure is dangerous. It invites blame, loss of authority, and public distrust. In a system with built-in correction, failure triggers process rather than punishment. This encourages early detection and reduces the incentive to conceal or rationalize misalignment.

Restoration does not require consensus on outcomes. It requires agreement on process. In pluralistic societies, disagreement is inevitable. The goal of governance is not to eliminate disagreement, but to prevent disagreement from paralyzing or destabilizing the system. By shifting conflict from ideology to structure, this framework allows opposing views to coexist within a shared discipline of review and correction.

Another advantage of restoration is continuity. Because institutions are preserved, institutional knowledge is retained. Expertise is not discarded. Capacity is not reset. Instead of burning down systems to rebuild them, restoration trims, realigns, and refines. This reduces disruption while increasing legitimacy.

Restoration also addresses scale. Large systems are difficult to reform because change feels risky. By emphasizing bounded authority, limited scope, and reversible action, this framework allows change to occur incrementally. Small corrections accumulate into large improvements without requiring comprehensive overhaul.

Critically, restoration restores trust not by demanding faith, but by demonstrating restraint. Trust grows when people see that power can stop, that programs can end, and that authority can expire without catastrophe. Nothing builds confidence like visible limits that are actually enforced.

The constitutional system was designed for this kind of maintenance. It assumes imperfection. It anticipates drift. It provides tools for correction. What it does not do is enforce their use automatically. That responsibility falls to practice, not text. This book argues that restoring practice is both possible and sufficient.

Restoration without revolution is not passive. It is disciplined. It requires leaders willing to accept limits, institutions willing to pause, and systems willing to be measured honestly. It requires abandoning the illusion that more action is always better than better action.

The result is not a smaller government or a larger one, but a more legible one. A system where purpose is stated plainly, authority is granted conditionally, execution is observable, and correction is expected. Such a system can evolve without losing itself.

The Constitution does not promise perfection. It promises durability through constraint. When its operating principles are followed, governance can adapt without collapse and correct without coercion.

The work of this book is not to inspire revolution, but to enable restoration.

The tools are already in place.

What remains is to use them.

CHAPTER 9 — Restoration Without Revolution

Citations and References

Constitutional Text

Declaration of Independence — Consent of the governed and right of redress through orderly means.

U.S. Constitution, Preamble — Government instituted to secure liberty through lawful structure.

U.S. Constitution, Article I — Legislative authority to grant, limit, renew, or terminate permission.

U.S. Constitution, Article II — Executive duty confined to faithful execution of law.

U.S. Constitution, Article III — Judicial enforcement of constitutional limits.

Amendment Process (Article V) — Structural change is deliberate and constrained, not reactive.

Supreme Court Precedent

Marbury v. Madison — Legitimacy preserved through judicial correction within existing structure.

Youngstown Sheet & Tube Co. v. Sawyer — Restoration of limits without institutional replacement.

INS v. Chadha — Structural violations corrected without rewriting the Constitution.

Bowsher v. Synar — Separation restored by enforcing existing boundaries.

Seila Law LLC v. CFPB — Accountability restored through constitutional enforcement, not redesign.

West Virginia v. EPA — Reassertion of limits using existing doctrine.

Statutory and Administrative Practice

Use of sunsets, reauthorizations, and appropriations to constrain authority.

Judicial invalidation of overreach followed by legislative redesign rather than replacement.

Institutional reform via rule withdrawal, scope reduction, and bounded delegation.

Restoration of oversight authority without expansion of power.

Historical and Empirical Record

Repeated constitutional corrections without amendment or regime change.

Historical reliance on enforcement of limits rather than institutional replacement.

GAO and Inspector General findings leading to redesign within existing agencies.

Demonstrated capacity for correction through restraint rather than revolution.

Proof of Coherence — Chapter 9

Claim

Governance alignment can be restored within existing constitutional institutions by reasserting restraint, rotation, and accountability, without amendment or revolution.

Falsifiability Condition

Evidence that durable alignment requires constitutional replacement, suspension, or extra-constitutional authority to correct systemic drift.

Supporting Authority

Separation of powers doctrine; repeated Supreme Court enforcement of limits; constitutional mechanisms for renewal and correction.

Observed Pattern

Structural drift is corrected through enforcement of existing constraints rather than institutional overthrow.

Status

Claim remains coherent. Constitutional practice confirms restoration without revolution.

CONCLUSION

Governance fails when it forgets how to return to restraint. This book offers no promises of perfect outcomes—only a system that detects error early, corrects honestly, and preserves legitimacy through clarity and constraint. That is coherence under law.

Throughout these chapters, the argument has remained deliberately narrow. This work has not attempted to define what governments should want, only how they should decide. It has not proposed new rights, new institutions, or new sources of authority. It has focused instead on order: the order in which meaning, authority, and action must occur if governance is to remain intelligible, accountable, and durable.

The central failure Identified is not corruption in the moral sense, nor incompetence in the administrative sense. It is the loss of restraint as an operating principle. When systems forget how to stop, they also forget how to learn. Momentum replaces judgment. Continuity replaces consent. Stability replaces alignment. Over time, governance becomes something that happens to society rather than something carried out on its behalf.

Restraint is the missing discipline. Not restraint as austerity or denial, but restraint as reversibility. A system that can stop can correct. A system that cannot stop must defend itself, regardless of outcomes. This distinction explains why so many reforms fail. They add layers of action without restoring the ability to pause. They promise improvement while entrenching drift.

The framework presented here restores restraint by restoring sequence. Meaning must come first, not as rhetoric but as a measurable claim about the world. Authority must follow, bounded in scope, duration, and review. Action must come last, observable and interruptible. When misalignment appears, the system must return to neutrality before moving forward again. This sequence is not optional. It is the condition of coherence.

Coherence under law does not mean uniformity or agreement. It means that disagreement occurs within a system capable of self-correction. In such a system, losing a debate does not mean losing legitimacy, because legitimacy is not derived from winning. It is derived from operating within constraint. When power is visibly limited, disagreement becomes survivable.

This is especially important in pluralistic societies. Consensus on values will always be partial and temporary. What must endure is the process by which decisions are made, tested, and revised. A coherent system allows opposing views to alternate influence without destabilizing the whole. Rotation replaces domination. Review replaces rupture.

Another theme running through this work is humility—not as a moral posture, but as a structural requirement. Systems that assume they will be wrong design for correction. Systems that assume they are right design for defense. The Constitution assumes error. That is why it embeds time, separation, and renewal. When these mechanisms are ignored or bypassed, the system loses its ability to adapt without shock.

Coherence also reframes success. Success is not permanence. It is fitness under current conditions. A policy that worked once may fail later. An authority that was necessary may become excessive. A program that delivered benefits may outlive its relevance. Coherent governance treats these transitions as normal rather than threatening. Ending something is not an admission of failure; it is evidence of alignment.

Importantly, coherence does not require omniscience. It does not require perfect data or flawless forecasting. It requires honesty about uncertainty and discipline in response. When outcomes diverge from intent beyond defined tolerance, the system must change. Not rhetorically, but structurally. This is the difference between explanation and correction.

The absence of this discipline explains why trust erodes even when institutions appear active. People do not lose faith because nothing is being done. They lose faith because they cannot see how decisions connect to results, or how failure leads to change. Trust grows when limits are visible and enforced. Nothing demonstrates accountability more clearly than the ability to stop.

This book does not claim that coherence will eliminate conflict, scarcity, or error. It claims something more modest and more important: that coherence makes conflict governable, scarcity debatable, and error survivable. It turns collapse into correction and crisis into review.

The constitutional system already contains the tools required for this discipline. Separation of powers, time-bound authority, reauthorization, and judicial limitation are not symbolic features. They are operational controls. When used consistently and together, they form a closed loop of legitimacy.

What has been lost is not the text, but the habit. Governance has drifted toward motion without pause, authority without expiration, and action without recalibration. Restoring coherence means restoring habits: stopping when thresholds are crossed, redesigning when meaning blurs, and validating only after correction is verified.

This is not a call for less government or more government. It is a call for legible government. A system whose actions can be explained, whose failures can be acknowledged, and whose power can be restrained without fear.

Coherence under law is not dramatic. It does not promise salvation or transformation. It promises something quieter and more durable: a system that knows how to return to itself.

That knowledge is what has been missing.

CHAPTER 10 — Coherence Under Law (Conclusion)

Citations and References

Constitutional Text

Declaration of Independence — Legitimate government derives authority from consent and exists to secure rights, not perpetuate itself.

U.S. Constitution, Preamble — Government purpose framed as ends, not mechanisms.

U.S. Constitution, Article I — Authority is conditional, temporary, and revocable.

U.S. Constitution, Article II — Execution is subordinate to law, not self-justifying.

U.S. Constitution, Article III — Judicial review preserves coherence by enforcing limits.

Fifth Amendment — Due process requires justification, reversibility, and reasoned decision-making.

Supreme Court Precedent

Marbury v. Madison — Legitimacy depends on the ability to invalidate unlawful action.

Youngstown Sheet & Tube Co. v. Sawyer — Power without authorization lacks legitimacy regardless of intent.

INS v. Chadha — Structural discipline is required even when outcomes seem beneficial.

Motor Vehicle Manufacturers Association v. State Farm — Reasoned explanation is necessary to preserve legitimacy after failure.

West Virginia v. EPA — Authority must be explicit, testable, and constrained to remain lawful.

Statutory and Administrative Practice

Judicial invalidation of action followed by lawful redesign rather than continuation.

Use of sunsets, expirations, and reauthorizations to restore alignment.

Withdrawal or narrowing of rules after failure to meet statutory purpose.

Oversight and audit mechanisms functioning as corrective rather than justificatory tools.

Historical and Empirical Record

Long-term erosion of public trust correlated with opacity and irreversibility of authority.

GAO and Inspector General reports identifying lack of corrective follow-through as a systemic risk.

Historical examples of institutional resilience through restraint rather than expansion.

Evidence that systems capable of stopping retain greater legitimacy over time.

Proof of Coherence — Chapter 10

Claim

Governance legitimacy is preserved not by perpetual action or perfect outcomes, but by the ability to return to restraint, correct error, and operate within constitutional limits.

Falsifiability Condition

Evidence that systems which lack reversibility, restraint, and correction maintain long-term legitimacy, trust, and alignment despite persistent failure.

Supporting Authority

Due process jurisprudence; separation of powers enforcement; constitutional design emphasizing renewal, limitation, and review.

Observed Pattern

Legitimacy erodes when authority becomes irreversible and opaque, and is restored when limits are enforced and correction is visible.

Status

Claim remains coherent. Constitutional history and institutional practice confirm restraint as the foundation of durable legitimacy.

MASTER SOURCE

Appendix A — Comprehensive Authority, Precedent, and Record

This master source consolidates all constitutional, judicial, statutory, and empirical authorities relied upon throughout the book. Individual chapters cite into this record. No argument is made here; this appendix exists solely as the evidentiary backbone.

I. Foundational Civic Texts

Declaration of Independence (1776)
U.S. Constitution
- Preamble
- Article I (Legislative powers and limits)
- Article II (Executive authority)
- Article III (Judicial authority)
- Article V (Amendment process)
Bill of Rights
- Fifth Amendment (Due process)
- Fourteenth Amendment (Due process and equal protection)
The Federalist Papers
- Federalist No. 47 (Separation of powers)
- Federalist No. 48 (Legislative overreach)
- Federalist No. 51 (Structural checks and balances)

II. Supreme Court — Structural, Separation, and Authority Cases
Marbury v. Madison
Youngstown Sheet & Tube Co. v. Sawyer
Brown v. Board of Education
INS v. Chadha
Motor Vehicle Manufacturers Association v. State Farm
Bowsher v. Synar
Morrison v. Olson
Clinton v. City of New York
Whitman v. American Trucking Associations
Hamdi v. Rumsfeld
Boumediene v. Bush
FCC v. Fox Television Stations
Free Enterprise Fund v. PCAOB
Utility Air Regulatory Group v. EPA
Department of Homeland Security v. Regents of the University of California

Seila Law LLC v. CFPB
West Virginia v. EPA

III. Administrative Law and Delegation Doctrine
Nondelegation Doctrine (historical and modern applications)
Chevron deference (origin, application, and contraction)
Major Questions Doctrine
Administrative Procedure Act (APA)
Reasoned decision-making standard
Arbitrary and capricious review

IV. Budgetary, Fiscal, and Authorization Records
Appropriations Clause jurisprudence
Continuing Resolutions (CRs) as fiscal normalization
Sunset and reauthorization mechanisms
Congressional Budget Office (CBO) baseline methodology
Office of Management and Budget (OMB) performance frameworks

V. Emergency Powers and Temporal Authority
National Emergencies Act
Authorization for Use of Military Force (AUMF) timelines
Public health emergency declarations
Patterns of serial renewal without redefinition
Judicial limits on indefinite emergency authority

VI. Oversight, Audit, and Empirical Sources
Government Accountability Office (GAO)
– High Risk List (multi-decade recurrence)
– Program performance audits
Inspectors General (IG)
– Repeated unresolved findings

– Authority persistence analyses

Congressional Research Service (CRS)

– Delegation and oversight reports

VII. Historical Patterns and Institutional Practice

Expansion of the administrative state

Normalization of exception-based governance

Post-crisis authority retention

Judicial correction following prolonged drift

Restoration through enforcement of limits rather than institutional replacement

---

Appendix Status

This master source is complete, expandable, and non-narrative. It functions as the authoritative reference layer for the entire manuscript and supports falsifiability, precedent analysis, and legislative review.

Applied Case Study

Emergency Authority and the Failure to Return to Neutrality

Context

Emergency powers are among the clearest environments in which the inversion of Meaning, Authority, and Flow can be observed. Emergencies justify rapid action, temporary suspension of norms, and expanded discretion. The constitutional expectation is that once the triggering condition subsides, authority retracts and governance returns to the Neutral Baseline.

Stated Meaning

The declared purpose of emergency authority is to address an extraordinary, time-limited condition that cannot be managed through ordinary processes. The intended outcome is stabilization of the emergency condition and restoration of normal governance.

Observed Sequence (Inversion)

In practice, emergency authority often follows this sequence:

Flow is deployed immediately (funding, enforcement, mandates).

Authority is extended through serial renewal.

Meaning is reinterpreted to justify continuation rather than reassessed.

The system moves from response to management without formal reversion to neutrality.

Misalignment Signal

Misalignment becomes detectable when:

The emergency condition no longer meets its original threshold.

Authority continues without redefinition of scope or necessity.

Flow persists independent of measurable emergency outcomes.

At this point, the system has entered a −1 state: authority and execution persist while meaning has drifted.

Required Reversion (0)

Under the framework presented in this book, the correct response is not escalation or narrative defense, but reversion:

Expansion pauses.

Authority is constrained to minimum harm-prevention functions.

The original meaning is restated or formally revised.

Metrics are reassessed against current conditions.

This reversion does not deny the original emergency. It acknowledges that the justification for continued authority must be current, not historical.

Correction Process

Correction would involve:

Explicit determination of whether the emergency condition still exists.

Redesign of authority if a different, non-emergency condition remains.

Transition from emergency powers to ordinary statutory mechanisms.

Time-bounded authorization with clear review cadence.

Verification and Validation (+1)

Only after correction is implemented and outcomes verified does validation occur. Validation is provisional and expires automatically if conditions change or variance exceeds tolerance.

Observed Outcome Without the Framework

Absent this sequence, emergency authority tends to normalize. Reversion does not occur. Correction is deferred. Review becomes symbolic. Eventually, legitimacy erodes—not because the initial response was wrong, but because restraint was never restored.

What This Demonstrates

This case illustrates that:

Failure is not the emergency response itself.

Failure is the refusal to return to neutrality once the response phase ends.

The framework does not prevent decisive action.

It prevents decisive action from becoming permanent authority.

Why This Matters

The legitimacy of emergency power depends entirely on its reversibility. A system that cannot stop emergency authority cannot distinguish necessity from convenience. The trinary framework makes that distinction operational.

About the Author

Dwight R Vaughn

Read more at https://memnora-spark-dwightvaughn103.replit.app.

www.ingramcontent.com/pod-product-compliance
Lightning Source LLC
LaVergne TN
LVHW090428210926
848480LV00002B/734
* 9 7 9 8 2 3 3 1 1 2 9 8 0 *